APPENDIX No.

GEOGRAPHICAL NAMES ON THE COAST OF MAINE.

BY REV. EDWARD BALLARD, SECRETARY OF THE MAINE HISTORICAL SOCIETY.

BRUNSWICK, MAINE, *July*, 1869.

SIR: In compliance with the proposals addressed to me June 30, 1868, I have the honor to present to you the following attempt at an examination of the geographical nomenclature of the coast of Maine, for the purpose of furnishing a list of the names of Indian origin, with their proper orthography, so far as it now can be ascertained, and their interpretation; and also names given by early settlers, or others coming from European shores; and when practicable the dates when these latter began to be used as terms of specific designation; and to add such historical notes as may be desirable for the further elucidation of the points thus brought into view.

In regard to the names derived from the language of the aborigines of this territory, difficulty arises from various causes.

The first is found in the changes produced by dialectic departures from the one original language. This language has been properly named the *Abnàki*, derived from the primitive words, *wañban*, *white*, and *ahki*, also written *auke*, land or *place*, forming the compound word *Wañbanahki*.[1] As the light of the morning, before the rising of the sun, was an object of great interest to the wild men of the woods, in the pursuit of their game or their foes, they applied the term *wañban*, in one of its definitions, to denote "the clear morning light;" and then to designate the part of the heavens where it first appeared. Thus, the compound word was used to signify the "east-land," and, as a consequence, it was also applied to distinguish the language. By usage and the tendency of that usage to diminish the number of syllables, especially by foreigners, the name has been shortened to *Abnaki*,[2] though the forms *Abenaki* and *Abenaqui* are sometimes used, with an equal respect for the origin of the name, which was not only adopted by the Indians of Maine, but was also applied to them by their fellow-natives living at the west of their territory.[3]

The name Algonquin has also been adopted to denote this language, which was not only the outlet of thought for the several tribes of the region now known as Maine, but served a similar purpose for all the tribes of New England, the new "Dominion of Canàda," and the chief parts of the present States lying north of North Carolina and Kentucky, and those in the Northwest beyond the Mississippi. Indeed, it may be said to have spread over all the North from the Gulf of St. Lawrence to the prairies of the West, with its northern limit bordered by the Esquimaux; excepting from its range the entirely distinct language of the *Hodénosaunee*, "The People of the Long House," known in our history as the Six Nations of the Iroquois[4] in New York, and the tribes residing on the borders of Lakes Erie, Huron, and St. Clair. This name *Algonquin* or *Algonkin* is taken from a small tribe in Canada,[5] and in this wide sense is of only a recent application.[6] It is convenient, as not being limited by a narrow geographical restriction like *Abnaki;* and may well be allowed to keep the place which Indian scholars seem willing to permit it to have.

[1] In pronouncing this word the Indians add the sound of *m* after the first *ñ*, which Râle introduces in the word *arañmkik*, "sous la terre;" and give a peculiar rush of guttural breath, not to be represented by letters.

[2] Râle's Dictionary of the Norridgewock dialect, Pickering's Preface, in Memoirs of the American Academy, Vol. I, new series, p. 372.

[3] Heckewelder, Hist. Acct. of Indian Nations, pp. 25, 107, 109, 111, who wrote *Wapanachki*.

[4] Morgan's "League of the Iroquois," 1851.

[5] Lescarbot speaks of the Etechemins, the Algoumequins, and the Montagnés as together sending a thousand men against the Iroquois. With an allowable liberty he writes the name differently from the now more common form. *Hist. Nouv. France*, Liv. III, ch. 10. Mass. H. Coll., 2d ser., X, 131.

[6] La Hontan, however, in 1715 gave more than thirty tribes as using this dialect. But his testimony is somewhat marred by including the Esquimaux in the number. Tome II, pp. 36–38.

But while this language is thus widely extended, and perhaps was once used as *one* throughout its whole domain, lapse of time, separation of tribes, diminished intercourse between them, various new circumstances, and the want of all power to fix the language with any approach to permanency by orthographic means, have produced changes in words to an extent that makes the dialects to appear even more than the dialects of ancient Greece, as if they were in reality different languages. As a single instance, reference may be made to the name of *hatchet*. In the Virginia dialect it was *Tamahaak*,[1] whence is derived the name tomahawk. In the Delaware it is *Temahican*. In the Penobscot dialect in Maine it is *Tàmhegan*. In the Norridgewock it is *Temahigan;* in the Micmac, *Tumhegn*. In other words, the variations have become so great that the Indians of the tribe at Oldtown on the Penobscot, and their brethren of the Passamaquoddy tribe at Pleasant Point, though not a hundred miles apart, have great difficulty in conversing with each other; and both these have still greater in understanding the Micmacs of Nova Scotia. If the Norridgewocks, the Sokokis, the Souriquois, the Tarratines, the Etchemins, the Marasheets, and the Almouchiquois, were still as once living in the State, there would be a large measure of the same kind of impediment to intercourse still remaining. Yet their ancestors in remote days had the same language.

In the orthography of the names as well as in their interpretation, a knowledge of the different dialects is required. The means of gaining this knowledge is supplied in part by the labors of the missionaries of early times; among whom Râle is a memorable example of intelligence and fidelity.[2] They have reduced some of the dialects to a written form for the purposes of devotion, with translations. In words which conform to the dialects of Massachusetts and Rhode Island, the labors of Eliot, Cotton, and Roger Williams afford great assistance. Vocabularies of the Delaware, Virginia, and Western dialects also contribute valuable aid.

Another difficulty is found in the *forms* in which these geographical names appear. The Indians knew nothing of writing beyond certain attempts by figures of objects, drawn on the bark of the white birch and prepared skins, to indicate their movements on the march, and record their successes and defeats.[3]

Their words, as caught by the ear of the early navigators and the hardy pioneers in the forest, are presented in different orthographies. In some instances the change has been so great that the original form of the names has been nearly lost, and could not have been recovered but from the fact that the present Indians often retain the ancient name, and thus enable the inquirer to preserve it in accordance with their own expressions. And yet in some instances they do not entirely agree in their own utterances. We find a variation in pronunciation among them, as we also find it in that of our own language. As a single instance, the following changes of the word *oolegan*, *good*, are all equally well understood by the members of the present Penobscot tribe: *Ooregan*, *oolegan*, *owlegan*, *owregan*, *wunnegan*, *winnegan*, *wauregan*, *waulegan*, and perhaps some others. When to this variety of pronunciation there is added the imperfect writing of the early settlers and interpreters, a reason readily appears why the names of persons and places should be clad in several varying forms. In many cases where the existing vocabularies do not afford aid, the present Indians are unable to give an explanation. They refer them to an older language; and this must mean the original language, before it was broken into dialects, where changes have proceeded so far as to show an appearance of a language of a different structure; though the careful student will see the traces remaining sufficient to carry his thoughts back to the common parentage. Or they ascribe them to the temporary influence of other tribes, in fixing some of their words as permanent designations of certain localities.[4]

In determining the meaning of words, necessary aid is found in remembering that the Indians

[1] The word appears to be a compound, from *tehemen*, *to cut*, and *haac*, pronounced *hauc*, an *implement*, *tool*.

[2] His dictionary of the Norridgewock dialect was captured by Colonel Westbrook in 1721. 2 Williamson's Hist., 108. It is preserved in the library of Harvard University, and was published (1833) in the "Memoirs of the American Academy," Vol. I.

[3] The Micmacs had a hieroglyphical mode of writing, different from the pictographic, and somewhat like the Chinese, in which characters represented words and combined ideas. The early missionaries adopted the method and carried it onward to a large extent. New York Hist. Magazine, vol. 5, pp. 289–292. "Micmac or Recollect Hieroglyphics."

[4] The name *Chesuňcook*, denoting a large lake in the northern part of Maine, is one of this class. The Penobscot Indians do not explain it. But with the vocabulary of the Pennacooks, as given by Potter, in the Farmers' Monthly Visitor, Vol. XIII, 323, the meaning is ascertained to be *Great Goose Lake*.

of different tribes, and indeed to some extent in the same tribe, interchanged certain consonantal sounds without any hinderance to the communication of their thoughts. Thus the letters *b* and *p*, *l* and *r*, were used for each other; so were *k*, *g*, and *q*; and *t* was sometimes the substitute for *k*, and even for *q*; while *f* and *v* were not used in Maine, though sometimes appearing in the words as *written* by the new-comers; especially in the case of the latter of these two where *u* and *v*, in the old English custom, were employed as equivalents, as in the name applied to a locality in Maine, and afterward to a large part of its coast—*Mau-oo-shen*, written *Mav-oo-shen*. The Micmacs seem of late to have introduced *f* and *v* in place of *b*. Vowels were easily changed; and the persons who early wrote their words used much liberty in the introduction of such letters as they deemed best for their purpose; and through carelessness allowing *u* to appear as *n*, and the reverse. Letters were also introduced for the sake of avoiding harshness of sound, particularly in the composition of words,[1] formed by taking parts of several and "agglutinating" them into a new form; sometimes taking only a single sound or syllable from the least important, and sometimes extending the union to a length like the following:

"Nukkitteamonteanitteaonganunnonash."[2]

In the termination of words denoting *place*, the syllables *at*, *et*, *it*, *ut*, *set*, frequently appear; and, while used as affixes, have the power of prepositions, meaning *at*, *in*, *near;* also *ak*, *ek*, *ik*, *ok*, *uk;* and *ag*, *aug*, *og*, *ook*; and with *c* euphonic prefixed, *cook*, sometimes becoming *kuk*, *onk*, and *unk* with *l* prefixed, *lunk;* and some others, which will easily be seen to fall within this class, usually called *locative* affixes, such as *eag*, *keag*, *keak*, *ke*, *ki*. Sometimes syllables added appear to have been the termination of a verbal form for the purpose of giving a verbal meaning to the noun to which it is applied. Though they had no substantive verb, they seem to have had some idea of its nature; and by this addition they conveyed the thought of the object *existing* in the place to which they appropriated the name. But the more common derivation for these affixes will be found in the word *auké*,[3] *land, earth, place;* written in dialectic differences *ahki*,[4] *ohki*.[5] The first syllable under euphonic influences readily passed into *uk*, *ook*, and the other forms above noted, easily recognized as having their origin in this word, and as prevalent among the Massachusetts tribes, and those of its contiguous territory;[6] while in the central and eastern parts of Maine, the *last* syllable was frequently adopted for this use, appearing as *ki*, *ke;* and with *k* as a suffix, having the power of a preposition, making *kik;*[7] and from this, in the English mode of writing, becoming *keag;* which form also appears in other parts of New England. Sometimes, too, from the instinctive desire for euphony, the first consonant *k*, in which the meaning resides, was allowed to disappear, or be supplemented by another, and so was changed to *eag*, *deag*, *seag*, and others.

As the pine-tree was the characteristic growth of a large part of the State, it was but a natural consequence that many localities should be named with reference to this fact. The same is true in regard to the places frequented by the bear. Noted places for catching and drying fish were marked with names to designate these occupations. Thus we see the reason for the frequent occurrence of the same words in the interpretation of these names.

This attempt to explain the following words, as well as to present them in a correct orthography, is the first that has been thus systematically made. In the majority of them there can be

---

[1] "This language doth greatly delight in *compounding of words*, for abbreviation, to *speak much* in *few words*, though they be sometimes *long;* which is chiefly caused by the *many syllables* which the *Grammar Rule* requires, and *suppletive syllables* which are of no signification, and curious care of *Euphonie*." Eliot, Ind. Gram. in Mass. Hist. Collections, 2d ser., Vol. IX, p. 252.

[2] The language of the Esquimaux is even more prolific in long words. The expression "Lest I be full," (Prov. 30, 9,) is thus translated: "Karsillârnekârnàuviæ̀issegallóartonga." But an example by J. Hammond Trumbull, to whose eminent success in Indian scholarship the present writer is much indebted, furnished in a note to his edition of Roger Williams' Key, p. 184, and lengthened beyond all that has yet appeared, "gives, in illustration of 'the Indian way of compounding words,' one of twenty-two syllables, which signifies 'our well-skilled looking-glass makers:'

"*Nup-pahk-nuh-tô-pe-pe-nau-wut-chut-chuh-quô-ka-neh-cha-e-nin-nu-mun-nô-nôk!*

"One can hardly look at it without stammering. With a language permitting the construction and use of such compounds as this, the 'man of few words' might yet be loquacious."

[3] R. Williams.

[4] Schoolcraft.

[5] Eliot.

[6] As *ak*, *ok*, *oc*, *og*, *aug*.

[7] Râle's Dict., "Terre." But *auké* is here sometimes retained: as in *K'tahdenauké*, now Mt. *Katahdin;* *howanochewauké*—white man's place, *i. e.*, house.

but little doubt as to a near approach to accuracy in both particulars. Some are involved in an obscurity which further investigation may remove.

A few English local names, as before mentioned, are added for the purpose of referring to their origin, and, as far as may be, to the times and reasons of their application to localities well known.

Trusting that this effort to illustrate the geographical names on the coast of Maine, as to their orthography, meaning, and history, will be acceptable and prove beneficial to your Department, I have the honor to be, very respectfully, your obedient servant,

EDWARD BALLARD.

Prof. BENJAMIN PEIRCE, *L.L. D.*,
Superintendent U. S. Coast Survey.

GEOGRAPHICAL NAMES ON THE COAST OF MAINE.

ABAGADUSSET.—This name is given to a river and a point on the north side of Merrymeeting Bay. The original name of the point was *Nagusset.*[1] At a later day it was called "Point Agreeable." Among its several forms occurs *Bagadasset;* which agrees with the word *bagadassek*, given by Râle under *eclairer* to *shine;* who also under *soleil* gives *pagadassem, il eclaire, i. e.*, the sun shines. It is not known whether the river or the Indian chief of early days first received this name, which was probably taken from the reflection of the sunbeams on the waters of this broad inland bay. This sagamore, jointly with Kennebis, of Swan Island, deeded land to Christopher Lawson, of Boston, October 8, 1649, who built a house and dwelt on the western side of the Kennebec, below the bay, and afterward sold to Thomas Lake, but in such a way as to be deemed to have conveyed no title.[2] This chief appears to have been peaceful, like "The Shining Sun."

But another mode of writing the word *Abeguaduset*, suggests a preferable interpretation, from the word *begwâtus*[3] *bay.* It may refer to the large expanse of Merrymeeting Bay, or to the broad opening of the river bearing the name at the head of this article. Dropping the first letter, probably an English prefix, and using the locative *et*, the word finds its equivalent in *At* the Bay, as the place where the chief has his home.

ACQUEHADONGONOCK.—This word denoted a point on the west side of the "Chops," *Kebec*, where the Kennebec leaves Merrymeeting Bay in its progress to the ocean. It is derived from *Ughiadi*, to finish, terminate; *agiwañn, dried*-fish, (Râle,) *augowam* and *auguan*, (John Smith,) *smoked fish*, and *ock*, a *place.* The full form will, therefore, be *Ug-hi-ad-an-gwañ-ock.*[4] The form given at the head of this article is found in the ancient maps of the Pejepscot Company, now in possession of the Maine Historical Society. The accepted interpretation of the name is Smoked-Fish-Point.

AGAMENTICUS.—This name was given by the Indians to the stream now called *York River*, at the mouth of which Sir Ferdinando Gorges planned to found the city which was called "Gorgeana," and incorporated by him by a grant in 1642. Thence it was appropriated to the mountain near its source, called by Captain John Smith "Sassenowe's Mount," and by the Prince his Highness, "Snodon Hill." It is derived from the form of the little pond in the town of Eliot, at its head, which is much like that of the Indian snow-shoe, *añghem*, plur., *anghemak.*[5] The last syllable is the same as *koos*, a stream, from *kesoose*,[6] to *run*, or *koosihada*,[7] to *run* down. The full form of the word, therefore, was *An-ghem*-ak-koos, with the euphonic syllable *ti* interposed to make *An-ghem-ak-ti*-koos, meaning "Snow-shoes River," or "Raquette River," as in the Adirondack region of New York. By the softening process of usage it has come through various orthographies to its present form, *Agamenticus.*[8]

ANDROSCOGGIN.—The present form of the name borne by this important river, improperly

---

[1] So says tradition, confirmed by documents in the Pejepscot Papers, Vol. 1, p. 105. S. Davis, p. 491[a], Cossen's deposition. Maps in same, 50 and 54[a], 1719.

[2] Pejepscot Papers, Vol. 1.

[3] See Castine.

[4] *Ock*, or *auk*, from *auke*, land.

[5] Râle under *raquette lac.* When a bay in a lake was described, the word was *wañriañghemak.* The word is derived from *añgmakou*, the ash-tree, of which wood the curved rim was made.

[6] In the *Kimzooi Awikhigan.*

[7] Râle under *avaler.*

[8] John Smith wrote it *Accominticus. Ahkeekwontep. Seal Head* on Fox Islands; *ahkeek-seal, upakwontep, head.*

reports its original, *Amoscougan*, as it appears in "The Indian Perepole's Deposition."[1] It has been thought to have been given in compliment to Governor Andros,[2] who had taken an active interest n the affairs of Maine for several years, beginning as early as 1677. But the name appears in an instrument for the conveyance of the right of sovereignty over a large tract of land on both sides of the river, from the falls at Brunswick, by Thomas Purchase, to John Winthrop of Massachusetts, in 1639. Perhaps the influence of Andros in the province had the power to perpetuate his name in this connection successfully over the other sixty forms in which it has been written, according as its sound was received by the ancient hunters, owners, and settlers. There seems to have been a disposition to make it conform to known words in the English usage. The name "Coggin" is a family appellation in New England; and it was easy to place before it, according to each man's preference, other familiar names, and to call the stream "Ambrose Coggin," "Amos Coggin," "Andrews Coggin," "Andros Coggin," and "Andrus Coggin." Its derivation is from the word *namās, fish*, abbreviated, as is the frequent practice, by dropping the first letter, and *skaouhigan*, (*skowhegan*,) a fish-spear. Under the word *poisson*, Râle gives *kankskaouihigan* as a *trident*, or the long piece *of iron in the middle of it*. The last part of this word denotes the iron point between the two outer portions, each of which is called *ĕnegahquok*. The syllable *kaňk* is the line that draws the flexible sides together.[3] This part of the word is retained as a local name originally applied to the falls at *Skowhegan*, on the Kennebec, just below which the waters have long been frequented for torch-light *spearing*.[4] The name, as furnished by Perepole with his description, marked the part of the river above the *Amitigonpontook*—that is, the "Clay-land Falls" at Lewiston; upward to "Arockamecook"—that is the "Hoe-land," at Canton Point. The rips and shallows in this portion were favorable for *spearing fish* beyond any part below. The name may, therefore, be translated the *Fish Spear*, or Fish *Spearing*.[5]

ATKINS' BAY is the expanse of water near the mouth of the Kennebec, between Hunniwell's Point, on which Fort Popham stands, and Cox's Head. It takes its name from an owner of the adjoining territory, who was an original settler,[6] and afterward sold his property to William Cock,[7] in 1662, consisting of 1,300 acres of land, of which the first existing map was made in 1731.[8] It is without doubt the aboriginal *Sabino*, which will be explained in its proper place. Mr. Atkins had ten daughters, and the fact that in the transfer of property after his decease they all signed the deed with their marks shows the studied inattention to female education in the laws of Massachusetts, from the south shore of which State Mr. Atkins came, and to which he appears to have removed after the sale of his land.

BEDABEDEC,[9] (*Be-da-be-da-ki.*)—The original name of the region about "Owl's Head." The word is first seen in Champlain, who describes it as "a low land," (*une terre basse*,) and the cape as "La Pointe de Bedabedec." The derivation of the name is somewhat conjectural; but it appears to come from *nĕbe, water*, abbreviated and repeated; *da*, interjectional, *there*, to indicate admira-

[1] Maine Hist. Coll., Vol. III, 333, taken from the Pejepscot Papers, Vol. 1, 504a. Perepole is Pierre-Paul.

[2] Webster's Dictionary, p. 1629.

[3] Compare *skahaňgan, bois fourchu*, in Râle, and *skahogan*, a "forked post," in "Kimzowi Awikhigan," the *o* having a nasal sound; *sekowhegan* in Penobscot and *sequahegan* in Micmac is the iron *spike*, formerly bone.

The application of the parts of this word will be more apparent from the following representation of the spear as used now. The wooden triangular pieces of wood open upon the springs when pressed on the fish, and the iron spike pierces him. As the triangles spring back the line is drawn and he is secured.

[4] Lithgow's Deposition. Pej. Pap., Vol. 1.

[5] In an account of places on the coast and interior, with their names and distances, Purchas gives *Mas-sa-ki-ga*, which, from its position in his statement, was on the Kennebec. The full form of the word would be *Na-mās-sa-ke-gan*, (*namās, fish*.) This is sufficiently like the present name to show the nearness to certainty that it denoted the same locality as the present name of the falls on the Kennebec at *Skowhegan*.

[6] He attended a meeting for settling a government on the Kennebec, May 23, 1654. Hazard's Coll., I, 585.

[7] From him came the name Cock's Head, now Cox's.

[8] Pej. Pap., Vol. 6, Map 52.

[9] Ch. III, p. 62, edit. 1632. See Jeffery's maps. Champlain speaks of the mountains of "Bedabedec," p. 67, evidently meaning the Megunticook Range at Camden, called by Colonel Church, in his Indian Wars, "The *Mathebestuck* Hills," and by John Smith, nearer the beginning of the same century, (1614,) *Mecaddacut*, "against whose feet doth beat the sea." Mass. Hist. Coll., 3d ser., Vol. VI, 117. Church's narrative, 141. 2, Williamson, 95.

tion, repeated for emphasis, and *ki*, land or *place; water-there! water-there! place;* which in our language may find its proper expression in "Cape of the Waters" or "Cape of the Ocean." The Indians translate "Owl's Head" into *Co-co-cas-wantep-uk*, from *co-co-cas*,[1] *owl*, (*kookookasoo*, *chat huant*, Râle,) and *up-pak-wantep*, head, and *uk*, a locative. On Smith's map of 1614 it is "P. Travers."

BUNGANUNGANUCK, commonly shortened to *Bunganuck*.—This small stream, flowing into Maquait Bay, runs at the bottom of a deep ravine, the deepest for a long distance on this part of the coast, and on this account became to the natives a fit object for a special designation to indicate that feature. In one of the cognate dialects the word *Pank-han*-nunk denotes *under the bank*, from *pank-han-ne*, a *bank*. *P* and *b* are often interchanged, and vowels oftener. Thus this word receives an explanation in perfect accordance with the high and steep *banks* on both sides of the stream, which seem to be more emphatically described by the repetition of the syllables *ungan*.[2] It may be represented in English by "High-bank Brook."

CAPE ELIZABETH.—The date of the discovery of this cape, and the person by whom the name was given, are not known. The first appearance of the name is on John Smith's map, 1614. The Indian name was *Apistama*.[3] The present one may have been given by Gosnold in 1602, or Pring, more probably in 1603. Gorges reports of him that he "brought with him," on his return, the most exact discovery of the coast that has since come into his hands.[4] The Queen reigning at the commencement of that century has her name here permanently fixed on this prominent headland of Maine.

CASCO, (*kasko*.)—This bay, early known as the *Archipelago* of Gomez,[5] bears a name easily interpreted. The word *kaskou* appears in Râle's dictionary under *oiseaux* without any equivalent In the "Kimzowi Awikhigan," *kasko* is *crane*, and the present Indians give the same explanation. In early maps and writers it appears as *Koskebee*, *Kaskebee*, *Cascobé*, which forms are easily resolved into *kasko-nebe*. The abbreviation of the last word, as is usual in composition, helps to make the word *Casco-be*, to be translated *Crane-water* or *Crane* Bay. An early name was *Aucocisco*, as seen in Smith; probably pronounced *Uh-cos'-is-co*, the first syllable being deeply guttural, and was written as the hearers caught the sound. The crane or heron still frequents these waters.[6]

CASTINE was named from the Baron de St. Castine, who occupied the place of the present remains of the old fort near the water of the bay, a short distance from the town, and on the spot where the Plymouth Company from Massachusetts had a trading establishment in 1626. D'Aulnay erected his fort some years later, (1635–'40.)[7] Castine came about 1665.[8] The place had been formerly known as *Bagaduce*, *Bigaduce*, and indeed by a variety of similar sounding names, among which Major Biguyduce, erroneously supposed to be the name and title of a French officer once a resident there, came nearer than the rest to the original.

Matche-be-gwâ-toos.—*Matche* is *bad*, and *be-gwa-toos* is *bay*. In the explanation by the Indians the name marks a place in the harbor of Castine, where, when the tides from different entrances meet over sunken rocks, the navigation is so difficult and perilous for their light canoes as to suggest the name of Bad Bay.[9] Purchas gives *Chebegnadose*, which omits the first syllable *mat*, and by an easy error gives *n* for *u*.[10]

CATHANCE.—This winding river runs into Merrymeeting Bay on the north side. The word *ka-*

[1] Zeisberger, in the Delaware dialect gives *gŏk-hos*, *g* for *c*.

[2] Eliot, Gram. p. 17. R. Williams, Key, Trumbull's note, 208.

[3] Williamson's Hist., Vol. 1, p. 30, note. It was also called by the Indians *Semiamis*, R. H. Major's note in Strachey. Caput IX, Aug. 28, 29. These two names were probably attached to two different points of the same projection.

[4] Brief Narration, Ch. V. The way in which Smith, and after him (Levett,) in 1623, introduce the name, shows that this cape was already a recognized point, (Me. H. Coll., Vol. II, p. 86.) The death of Elizabeth, in 1603, would seem to be a reason for the naming of the point by Pring, rather than by Smith many years later. See Smith, Mass. H. C., Vol. VI, 3d ser., and Map, Vol. III, 3d ser.

[5] Me. Hist. Coll., 2d ser., Vol. I, p. 299. Ribero's map, 1529.

[6] Willis' Hist. Portland, p. 15.

[7] Williamson's Hist., I, 308.

[8] Me. Hist. Coll., Vol. VI, p. 111.

[9] Râle "noms" writes it "Matsibigwadoosek, la riviere, ou est Mr. St. Gastin;" the word is the *same*, *matsi*, *bad*, with the locative *ek*.

[10] Pilgrimage, Vol. IV, p. 1674.

thans in Quinnipiac dialect of Connecticut is translated *seas.*[1] But this supplies no aid here. The word is explained by the Indians as *bent, crooked.* They pronounce it *Kat-hah-nis.* Another river of the same name is found in the eastern part of the State, near Dennysville, of the like winding character.

CHÁMCOOK is the name of a short range of mountains in New Brunswick, on the eastern side of the St. Croix, which takes its name from the narrow part of the river, known to the natives as *K'tchamcook,* from *k'tche,* great, the abbreviated *namas, fish,* and the locative *cook.* The meaning is *the great fish-place,* of which the reputation still continues.

CHEBEAG, erroneously written *Gebeig, Jebeig.*—The analysis of the full word would be *k'tche, great, nebe,* abbreviated *water,* ak, a locative, making *K'tchebeak, Great water-place.* From the heights of this large island the ocean view is very extensive.

CHEPUTNATICOOK.—This name of the upper part of the St. Croix is probably taken from one of the boundary lakes. It has been said to mean Great-Hill Lake.[2] Its long and narrow form, like a wide river, is bordered on the west by a range of abrupt and elevated ridges, covered with a heavy "black growth," chiefly spruce, and might well suggest this explanation. But in dividing the word into its parts, *K'tche-put-natic-ook,* and finding in a cognate dialect the word *nataque, (nătăk,)* beaver, it would seem to refer to an abounding place for this animal. The second syllable, *put,* is still obscure, as is indeed the meaning of the whole word. It is often shortened to *Cheput-nacook* and *Cheputnook.*

CHEWONK, from *k'tche, great, w* euphonic, and *onk,* a locative, finds its equivalent in *Great Neck.*

CHICKAWAUKEE, a pond supplying the city of Rockland with water, *k'tche, great,* kooĕh, *pine, auke, place.* The first part of the second word is taken to make *K'tche-koo-auke,* representing *Great Pine Lake.*

COBSCOOK would be more correctly *Cob-os-se-cook*; from *cob'-os-se* or *cab'-os-se,* (kabassé, Râle,) and *cook,* a locative, equal to Sturgeon River. A similar name, *Cobossecontee* or *Cobosseconticook,* is the name of the mouth of the valuable mill-stream at Gardiner, where this kind of fish anciently abounded.[3] The stream itself was called Sq-uagŭset, implying that some important Indian dame had once dwelt on its banks.[4]

COX'S HEAD.—For the origin of this name see ATKINS' BAY.

COWSEAGAN.—This narrow passage near Wiscasset bears a name corresponding to the word *koussigan,*[5] denoting an Indian mode of kindling fires, with certain forms and ceremonies, for the purpose of foretelling future events or ascertaining about the absent in war or in the chase; whether they are living or dead. Perhaps this neighborhood was the place where this was often done. The Indians explain it as "Fortune-telling."

DAMARISCOTTA.—This was Tamescot in Heylin and other early writers. The present Indians call the river *Matamascontee;* a name also of a tributary of the Penobscot in the northern part of the State. They explain it in reference to successful fishing. The analysis of the word denotes that a certain kind of fish, at the proper season, were abundant in the tide-water below the steep falls, up which they went into the fresh-water pond, a short distance above, for increase. The component parts of the word are *mahdāmās, alewife,* and *kontee,* implying *plenty,* making *mahdamaskontee.* In the other stream of this name, this kind of fish has ceased to appear, being hindered by mill-dams below. The present name of the river and town, sometimes divided into two parts, seems to have been deduced from a desire to make the native words assume an English form. John Cotta married into the family of Richard Wharton, one of the large landholders in Maine, and received here a tract of land as the heritage of his wife. At an earlier date some one of the name may have resided on the river, or been well known as in traffic with the settlers on its banks. Possibly some one of the family may have borne the name of Damaris. At all events, the name *Damaris Cotta* was more agreeable than *Matamascontee,* or *Tamescot,* its abbreviation; and, thus gaining the

---

1 Trumbull's note in R. Williams' Key, p. 33. Note 18, in MS. letter referred to Eliot's *kehtahhanash, seas.* Neh. 9, 6.

2 Springer's Forest Trees and Forest Life in Maine, p. 179.

3 Lithgow's Dep. Hist. and General Register, Jan., 1870, p. 23, *where it* is *Cawbisseconteague,* and explained, "Sturgeon-land."

4 MS. map, supposed to have been made by Colonel Church, in reference to the "Second Indian War," 1688–97. It is preserved in the State Archives at Hartford, Connecticut.

5 Râle's Dict., *Jongleur, Jonglerie.*

ascendency, has prevailed to the present day. The family name of "Cotter" is found there still. The immense heaps, or rather hills, of oyster-shells, showing the action of fire, are a proof of the former abundance of this bi-valve in this stream, and the long continued visits or permanent dwelling of the Indians on both its banks. In Jackson's Geological Report the quantity is estimated at 44,906,400 cubic feet of shells, capable of producing 10,000,000 casks of lime of the usual dimensions.

DAMASCOVE, Damarin's Cove, or Damaris Cove, could hardly have been derived from Damaris-cotta, for the name "Damarill's Isles" is found in John Smith, (1614,) and suggests that these names had a different origin. The word seems to have included if not describing Pemaquid Bay.

DOUAQUET.—See JORDAN'S RIVER.

EBENECOOK, now the name of a harbor northwest of Southport Island, was probably the name of the island itself. If it were *Ebemécook*, and perhaps it was, it would mean *High-bush-cranberry-place.*

Ibemènécook means *Choke-cherry-place.* Another explanation may be suggested from the Passamaquoddy word *munigu*, an island, and *ook, place*, making *Muníquook*, or, as otherwise, *Menikŭk*, changing *m* to *b*. Thus it would be Běněcook, "The Island," easily changed to the present form.

EGGEMOGGIN, *Edgmoggin, Edgmorragen.*—A reach between Deer Island and the towns of Sedgwick and Brooklin. The Indian word *ăgămoggin, snow-shoes*, may be the correct explanation of this name, having some allusion to this "Reach" which is not now known.

FRENCHMAN'S BAY derived its name from the settlements on the grants made on its borders, to Mons. Cadillac, from Louis XIV, in 1691, to confirm the possession of what was claimed to be Acadia. His granddaughter, Madame Gregoire, in 1787, acquired from Massachusetts a partial confirmation of the original concession.

HARRISEEKET was the name of Freeport; probably denoting the broad part of the river nearest Casco Bay. The word *hallaseget* means to *cut* with a knife, and is used with regard to cutting fish. An Indian explains it as *Dress-fish-place.*

HIPPOCRASS, improperly Hypocrites, "spiced-wine,"[1] a name probably given to this island by jolly seamen.

HOCKOMOCK.—A story of the Indian times, connected with this headland, implies that the word means "devil." But the dialectic names for the "evil spirit" were *matsi-niwesko*, and *matta-dewando*, contracted to *tanto*. In the Massachusetts language, or rather dialect, it was *hobomock*. The present word should be written *Honckamock*, from *honck*, a *goose*, *am* euphonic, (unless it is an abbreviation of *namās*, fish,) and *ock, place*. As applied to the water, as would be natural, it is the equivalent of *Wild-Goose-Bay*. This is one of the words that show how the Massachusetts dialect, in the word *honck*, had an influence in Maine. Where in the Norridgewock for *goose* was *awérér*, in the Penobscot it is *wompato*, and in Etchemin, *wahbegeel.*

HOG.—The name of an island in Portland Harbor, shortened from *quohog*, or, as given in Webster's Dictionary, *quahaug*, the *round clam*. The word is often pronounced *co-hog*. In Massachusetts it was written *quauhaug*, and in Narraganset *po quau-hock*. Râle wrote *pe-kwa-hak*, which he applies to *oysters*. The original word is thought to mean "a tightly closed shell."

When Christopher Levett visited the waters now known as Portland Harbor, in 1623, he reported it as "Quack," probably with the broad sound of the vowel, and gave the place the name of York, where he intended to found a city.[2] One acquainted with the local pronunciation can easily see how the change was made from the original Indian word.

HUNNIWELL'S POINT.—The name of the person whose name is attached to the point of land between Atkins' Bay and the ocean, at the mouth of the Kennebec, appears in a document dated May 18, 1672.[3] The place where his house stood is indicated on a pen-drawn map among the Pejepscot Papers.[4] The cellar still remains.

ISLE AU HAUT.—This mountainous island received its descriptive name from Champlain, in 1605, when, with De Monts, he coasted from the St. Croix to Cape Cod. It has a small settlement

[1] Webster's Dict. Williamson's Hist., I, 56.

[2] Me. Hist. Coll., II, p. 84. Willis' Portland, p. 26.

[3] Me. Hist. Coll., V, 240. His name is there signed Ambrose Honeywell. His house was standing in 1731, owned by J. Lewis.

[4] Vol. 6, Map 52.[a]

on the northeastern side, and a few scattered houses in other parts. The old French mode of writing the last word was "hault." This form appears in the present usage of the residents in that region, who call it "The Isle of Holt." Williamson recognizes the same form. The Indian name, Soolĕcook, is translated *Shell Place*. Smith noticed this mountain-island as one of "the remarkablest" landmarks, and wrote, "The highest isle is Sorico, in the bay of Penobscot."[1] The word is the same with the one given above, with a dialectic change by the Coast Indians of *l* to *r*. With the proper termination it would be *Sorĭcoke* or *Sorĭcook*.

ISLESBORO'.—Of this the Indian name is *Betowbagook*, which denotes its position between two channels.

JEREMISQUAM.—The Indians sometimes had English names given them by the early settlers and missionaries. In this region there were Sheepscot John, Robin Hood, (Darumkin,) Daniel Robins, (Ninemewet.) This name marks the name of one who bore that of the melancholy prophet, with the word *wigwam*, *house*, shortened by the English comers to *guam*, and then softened to its present form. *Jeremys-House* in this new mode was made to extend its name to all of Westport.

JORDAN'S RIVER, north of Mount Desert, and connected with Frenchman's Bay, was originally *Douaquet*, of which the meaning is not ascertained.

KEBEC is the same as Quebec, the French form of the word, meaning *narrows*.[2] Here it denotes the passage, where the Lower Kennebec leaves Merrymeeting Bay, called "The Chops." This name appears on a pen-sketched map, made about 1690, preserved in the archives of Connecticut, at the State-house at Hartford, and supposed to have been drawn from memory and conjecture by Colonel Church, as an aide to the commissioners of New England in preparing for the Indian war about that time. In Perepole's Deposition,[3] referred to under "Androscoggin," it is given *Quăbăcook*. This is the same word with the addition of the locative *ook*.

KENNEBEC.—Of the thirty different forms in which this name has been written, *Kennebekĕ* is probably the most correct. Divided into its parts, it will be *kenne* or *quenne*, *long*, *nebe*, *water*, *ke*,[4] *from*. The meaning is "*From the long water*," that is, "Moose Head Lake," which on Mitchell's map is called *Chenebesic*, or *Great Lake*. Its characteristic is length rather than breadth.

KENNEBUNK[5] is of similar origin with the foregoing; *kenne*, *long*, abbreviated to *ken*, *nebe*, *water*, and *unk*, a locative, *Long-water-place*, and properly so named, as the opening of the Kennebunk River is much the largest bay and best harbor for some distance on the coast.

KOWAHSKITCHCOOK.—There is a difficulty in knowing what is the proper word here to denote Machias River. It is called *Kowasskitchcook*, and this would mean *Pines-great-place*, referring to the upper falls. Also, with more probable correctness, *Kwapskitchcook*, which the Indians call *Rocky River*, to the two falls on which this designation is appropriate. The word *penops*, *rock*, will furnish a part of the first syllable, *k'tche*, *great*, the second, and the last is the locative. *Kw* is obscure, perhaps for *kooé*, *pine*. But *kowopscoo* means sharp-rock-ridge. This may refer to the sharp rocks in the rapids.

LEJOK is a name appearing on a map in Jeffrey's collection, near Blue Hill Bay. The name is remembered in the neighborhood, and some years ago it was given to a ship built at Ellsworth by Mr. Black. In one of the cognate dialects *lechauwak* denotes a *fork*. Perhaps it was applied here to mark two diverging branches of these waters.

MACHIAS.—The original word was *Machisses*, properly *Matchesis*, from *matche*, *bad*, and *sis*,[6] diminutive. *Bad*, *little*, i. e., *place* or *falls*; and was properly applied here, because, by reason of

---

[1] Description of N. E., 3d ser., Mass. H. Coll., Vol. VI, 120.

[2] *Kebec*, qui est un détroit de ladite riviere de Canada. Lescarbot, Vol. II, Ch. XIV, p. 307-(327.)

[3] Me. Hist. Coll., Vol. III, p. 333.

[4] Râle, p. 554, (18, 19.) He gives, ("noms" p. 493,) *Aghenibekki*, la riviere *Aïmesoukkanti*, which is a branch of the Kennebec, taking its name from the falls at Farmington, written on an ancient map in the Pejepscot Collection, Vol. 6, Map 50, 1719, *Amosequonty;* also elsewhere written in a dozen different ways, of which *Amasaconticook* is the one to be preferred, denoting Fish-plenty Place. The stream is "Sandy River;" in the Indian translation, *Penobsquisumquiseboo*. It is not easy to understand what meaning Râle's brief note is intended to convey. The present name is like the earliest, having been called *Kinibequi* by Champlain, in 1605-'6, and Biard, in his relation in 1611. Perhaps a thorough analysis of *Aghenibékki* would show it to mean a tributary to this main river.

[5] In Folsom's "Saco," from an old MS., *Kennibonke*.

[6] Vetromile's "Alnambayuli Awikhigan," 443.

the very narrow, winding passage between the crags of the water-course at the lower falls, no canoe could pass through. *Bad-small fall* contrasts it with the larger one about seven miles above, at what was probably the *Kwapskitchcook, Mahjais*,[1] which is but a different writing for *Machias*, is explained by *Bad-way.*

MAGOCOOK.—A bay extending from the mouth of Freeport River (Harriseeket) to Flying Point.

MAGUNCOOK, the early name of "Mousam River,"[2] has the same origin and meaning as *Meguntícook.*

MAQUAIT, from *maqua*, a *bear*, and the locative ending, *it. Bear-Bay* will well represent the meaning of the word, and the presence of this animal in its neighborhood in early days; though more strictly it may show where the natives went *at the bear.*

MATINIC.—John Smith mentions the three isles and a rock of *Matinnack.*[3] The name may possibly be explained like the next. Another form of the word is *Metenic.*

MATINICUS.—Smith refers also to this island, and says, "Metenicus is also three plain isles and a rock betwixt it and Monahigan."[4] The Indians call it *K'nahgook*, and explain it as "Long Island." This word may be from *kenne, long*, and the locative termination *cook.*

The one or the other of these two neighboring islands appear in the history of this coast as early as 1609, the year after the colony under George Popham, at the mouth of the Kennebec, broke up and returned to England. In that year his fort, St. George, was re-occupied by a company engaged in fishing, under a leader who treated the Indians with much harshness and injury. In retaliation for severities such as they had never received from the kind treatment of Popham, they took advantage of a favorable opportunity, killed a portion of the English, and by their intimidations compelled the rest to abandon their enterprise here, and select a new point for their efforts, at a place which they called Emmetanic. In 1611–'12 Captain Plastrier, in the French service, in attempting to go to the Kennebec, was taken prisoner by the English, with two ships, and carried to their station, "at an island called Emmetanic,"[5] thus asserting English supremacy in these waters. This name, and the occupation for which the English sought this island, leads to a partial indication of its meaning; *Amatanic* suggests *namās, fish;* the next syllable *tan* may come from *otan*, in the Narraganset dialect,[6] and *odāne* in the Norridgewock, meaning village. The name "Fish-Town" will not be inappropriate to the location. The terminal syllable in *Matinicus* is not explained.

MAWOOSHEN.—This was a name by which a part of the coast of Maine east of Cape Elizabeth[7] was known to early writers, some of whom wrote it *Mavooshen*, (*v* for *w*,) *Mawoshen, Moasham*, and *Mawashen.* This last mode nearly corresponds with the Penobscot word *maweeshen*, which, with a common locative, denotes *Berry-place*, descriptive of several localities near the coast; *Maweeshenook.*

MEDOMAC.—Also written *Madaamock* and *Madahumic.*[8] This variation suggests the form *Matta-am-ock; matta-not, namās, fish, ock*, place; implying the part of the river where the ocean *fish* are not found, as not being able to pass above the tide-water over the *falls* called *Chegewunnussuck*,[9] just above the village of Waldoboro.

MEDUNCOOK.[10]—A tide-river separating Cushing from Friendship, and connected with Muscongus Bay.

MEGUNTICOOK.—One of the Camden Hills, taking its name from the small river with falls near its base. The word is elsewhere found as Ammequunticook, resolvable into *namās, fish, konte*, plenty, *cook-place;* and may be uncouthly rendered as *Fish* plenty river. The Indian village near

[1] Cadillac, Memoir in the Hist. Coll., Vol. VI, p. 279, says: "Majais.—The entrance of this river is difficult on account of rocks, which are concealed at high water." The difficulty, however, is at the falls.

[2] Williamson's Hist., I, 26.

[3] In Mass. H. Coll., 3d ser., Vol. VI, 120.

[4] *Ibid*

[5] Caryon's edition of the Reports of the Jesuits. 1864, Paris.

[6] R. Williams' Key, p. 3, Râle, "Village."

[7] Gorges' "Brief Narration," B. II, Ch. VII.

[8] Pejepscot Papers. Records, I, 88; VI, map and paper of 1738.

[9] Pejepscot Maps. This word is also written *Magowmannussuck.*

[10] Williamson's Hist., I, 59.

the falls, "at the foot of a high mountain, against whose feet doth beat the sea," was known to John Smith as *Mecaddacut*, which represents the sound of the name as he caught it.[1]

MENAN, from *menahan*, *island*, by emphasis here, *The Island*, as being the largest, and on the maps "Grand Menan." In the Jesuit Relations it is called *Menano*, perhaps *Menanoke*.

MENÀNA, from the same word, with a suffix thought to denote separation, as *The Island*, separated from Monhegan. Smith wrote it *Monanis*, suggesting a diminutive, *Small Island*.

MERRICONEAG was originally applied to mark the "carrying-place" on Harpswell Peninsula or Neck, where a short space in one part of this long and narrow tract separates the waters of Casco Bay from those on the east side of this neck. It was often used in early times by the Indians, and is occasionally used by them at the present day. On the west side was a burial-place of the natives, which was discovered a few years ago in plowing, when several skeletons were exhumed, with wampum, copper ornaments, and axes of European make. An Indian company soon afterward passed across, and spoke of it as a well-known place for crossing, and knew of the burial-ground from long tradition. The word in full would be *Merrucoonegan*, from *merru*,[2] *swift*, *quick*, *c* euphonic, and *oonegan*, *portage*. As the portage at Winnegance was considerably longer and very steep, this, by contrast, could be well called *The Quick-Carrying-Place*.

MERRYMEETING BAY.—This name is said to have had two origins; one from the meeting of the waters of five rivers; and the other from a meeting of surveyors and their enjoyment of the occasion on its shores. But it may have been named from any other similar gathering at the house of the first settler, Thomas Purchase, about 1625–'28, or at any later time.

MONHEGAN.[3]—There is a difficulty in translating the name of this island, called St. George by Captain George Popham in 1607. Comparing it with the definition of Michigan, given by Schoolcraft, from a dialect of the language that reached to Maine, a clue may be found for its interpretation. *Mona*[4] and *munnoh*[5] mean *island*. *Mona-hegan*, changed by use to *Monhegan*, may perhaps mean "The Island of the Sea." Its position, if not this explanation, well entitles it to this distinction.

MONSEAG.—In the interpretation of the inscription on the Dighton Rock, *Chinkwalk*, at Mackinaw, gave to Schoolcraft *moris*, at the *loon*. The terminal syllable is for *place*, and the compound word may be rendered "Loon Bay," *Moosebeck*, or *Moosabeck*. There are other places on the eastern coast, in which the word *moose* occurs; as "Moose Cove," "Moose Neck." Perhaps this name is similarly formed, *moose-nebe-ki*, *i. e.*, *moosbeki*, to indicate the place where the animals came to the water. As this name was written by Colonel Allan, 1777, *Mispecki*, we have an aid for this form, which means *Moose-water-place*. But an Indian explains it thus: *Moosabekik*, a *wet place*; and as Râle, under *mouiller*, gives *mousabégat*, *it is wet*, and *ne-moussebegh-esi*, *I am all wet*, this must be taken as the more probable interpretation. But it requires an acquaintance with the locality to see its applicability to this narrow strait more than to other places. Perhaps there is a peculiarity in the tidal flow which made it a proper appellation.

MOUNT DESERT.—The Indian name of this island, as given by the natives in Biard's Relation, was *Pemetiq*, from *pemé'te*, *sloping*, and *ki*, *land*. It probably denoted a single locality, which the visitors understood as the designation of the whole territory. The vessel bearing him and his company made their first harbor at a place on the east side of the island, which they called St. Saviour, (Bar Harbor.)

In 1605 Champlain gave its several high elevations the name of "Monts Deserts," which well describes their barren appearance. They were doubtless seen by the earlier navigators, though not represented on their maps, unless under the general name of "les Montaignes," or "Montanas," on this part of the coast.

The earliest historical events on this island are those connected with Biard and his company of Jesuits in 1613, who were proposing to go to *Kadesquit*, (from *kaht*, micmac for *eel*, denoting *eel-stream*, now called *Kenduskeag*,) at Bangor, for the purpose of forming a religious settlement with a

[1] Third ser. Mass. H. Coll., VI, 117.

[2] Potter's Vocabulary.

[3] Also, among twenty other forms, *Menahiggin*, *Monàhigan*, (Smith.) The first refers the word to *menahan*, island.

[4] C. A. Potter on the language of the Pennacooks of New Hampshire.

[5] Eliot, Rev. 6, 14, etc.

missionary design, under the auspices of Madame de Guercheville, of Paris. While they were tarrying at their first harbor, they were visited by a party of Indians who persuaded them to make their abode at the home of Asticou, their chief, on the west side of Soames' Sound, at a place whose *sloping* surface toward the ocean renders it probable that this was the real *Pemetiq*. In the same summer Argoll, an English captain, with an armed vessel, had come from Virginia to procure the annual supply of cod-fish at the islands of Pemaquid. He there learned that the French had taken possession of territory claimed by the English under the charter of James, in 1606. He sailed thither immediately with authority from Governor Dale, of Virginia, for the purpose of their expulsion. With little resistance he captured the scarcely finished defenses and took all the company prisoners; whom he treated with a severity not at all needed to vindicate the claims of his government for the sovereignty. Here was the first blood spilled in the long contest between these two nations for supremacy on the North American continent.

The ocean views and the picturesque mountain scenery have made this island a favorite place of summer resort.

Its name in the Penobscot dialect is *Ahbăsauk*, which is the equivalent of *Clam-bake Island.* At the present day there are high banks of clam-shells near the mouth of Soames' Sound, from which the early settlers took away boat-loads to burn into lime. Similar banks are found at Hull's Cove, Indian Point, and several other places; reminding one of the oyster-shell banks at Damariscotta. The living clams are plentiful in all the coves of the island; and a considerable business is carried on at Bar Harbor and Indian Point, during the spring and autumn, in digging them for sale.[1]

The Indian tradition is that "long time ago, two, three hundred years or more," their ancestors gathered here for the purpose of feasting on this food. The facts in the case show their skill in fixing the name, which tells of their need and the enjoyment of their semi-annual visits to the place of their "clam-bakes."

MOUSAM, an English local name of the *Maguncook* River.

MUSCONGUS.—No explanation. Conjecture suggests *Moose-kon-koos*, or *mosq*, (a word for *bear*,) *kon-koos*.

NAGUSSET, the name of the point now called *Abagadusset*, (p. 246.)—*Nagusset*, the name of the point in Merrymeeting Bay now called *Abagadusset*, from *naaq*, a *corner*, a point of land.

NARRAGUAGUS.—The Indians do not explain this word. It may come from *nar-ah-e*, before, and *begwatoos*, the last *g* being changed to *t*, and the meaning may be *Before the Bay*, denoting Trafton's Island at its mouth.

NASKEAG, called by Smith[2] Nusket, which is probably a mistake for Nasket, as elsewhere written. As fishing was the employment of the Indians for half the year, it was natural for them to designate the places of their resort with the name of one of the principal means of their livelihood. Hence the frequent use of the word *namăs*,[3] in the composition of words. *Naskeag* is abbreviated from *Namaskeag*, or *kik*, and Nasket from *Namasket*, and represents *Fish-Point*, on Blue Hill Bay.

Namasket is also a place on Taunton River, in Massachusetts.

NEDDOCK.[4]—Hubbard gives it as Nidduck, and Jeffreys (Map 51) nearly follows him. It may be allied to *nitauke*, *my place*. In 1654 it was written Nuttake.[5] But a better interpretation has been suggested by the late Judge Potter, from the compound word, cited from Râle, *netegoo'ike*, *clear-land;* and confirmed by a leading Indian of the Penobscot tribe, in the word *nătuah*, an *intervale*. If the name be written *Net-ock*, the meaning, *cleared-land*, well corresponds with this projection, and its back-lying portion, and the many native implements found in cultivation. The Indians here seldom or never named a cape as such.

The large, irregularly shaped rock, separated by a narrow, navigable channel from the point of this cape, was noticed by Gosnold in 1602, when he saw here several Indians possessing articles of European manufacture; such as a Biscay shallop, with mast and sail, an iron grapple, a copper

[1] Letter from Hon. E. M. Hamor, of Mount Desert.

[2] On his map, *Lowmonds*, but in his list *Nusket*.

[3] Also written *namaes*, *namohs*, *namaas*, in different dialects.

[4] So Williamson writes it. Vol. 1, 24.

[5] Hon. E. E. Bourne, Kennebunk, MS. letter.

kettle, clothing of black serge, a hat and band, hose and shoes, blue cloth; and using words that showed that some Basques of St. John de Luz had been in the neighboring waters before him.[1]

NEQUASSET.—Cotton's vocabulary furnishes *nequt-tika* as *eel*. R. Williams supplies *mihtuck-quash-op*, as an *eel-pot*, the first part of the word denoting the wood of which it is made, and the last part its purpose. The similarity of these words to the name of this place may possibly be sufficient to warrant their union with the fact of the abundance of this kind of fish at the falls on this stream, at the head of the tide, and allow the explanation *Eel-Place.*

NEWAGEN.—The name of this cape has been singularly unfortunate in its orthography, appearing as *Anawagen*, *Andawagen*, *Bonawagen*, *Manawagen*, *Nawagen*, *Norwagen*, and *Caphan-of waggan*,[2] and several others. This variety creates a difficulty in the interpretation. Under the word *etroit*, Râle gives *ooskooaighen.* Perhaps the last three syllables enter into this word, which will thus represent the *Narrows* between the southern point of this cape and the adjoining islands. It is mentioned by Levett in his account of his voyage along the coast in 1623, who calls it Cape-manwagan.[3] Williamson says of the northern part, the island of Cape Newagen (now Southport) is separated from Booth-bay, to which it belongs, by a narrow passage for small vessels, called *Townsend Gut.*[4] This description goes far toward warranting the definition of the name here given. Off this cape Josselyn says is the place where Captain Smith fished for whales.[5]

NEW MEADOWS, originally *Stevens' River*, named from a resident on the south side of Merry-meeting Bay, whose house stood near the "carrying-place," about 1640 and later.

OGUNQUIT.—One of the forms of this word, in past days of frequent use, is *Negunquit*, and this suggests that the original was *Oonegunquit.* The word *oonegan* means a *portage*, *carrying-place*, and the termination *quit* denotes locality. The name *Portage-place*, or the *Portage*, conveys a proper designation of a singular ridge of beach-stones thrown up by the action of the ocean near the entrance of a short arm of the sea, to the height of about twenty feet, across which a carriage-road now passes.

OSSIPEE, from *kowâss*, *pines*, and *sēpē* river, *Pine River*, changed from k'wâs by dropping the first two letters.

PASSAQASSAWÂKEAG.—One interpretation of this word is the *Ghost-Place*, or Place of Sights, and the word *negwässankamawan*, *I see him*,[6] may be cited in its favor. Another explanation takes the word *Passagus*,[7] *sturgeon*, from the St. John's dialect.

PASSAMAQUODDY.—The various orthographies of the name of this bay receive the like interpretation. A Micmac Indian employed by the missionary at Hantsport, Nova Scotia, in translating the gospels, gave the word *Pestumacadie.*[8] Another form is the Etchemin, *Pascatumacadie.*[9] The uniform translation is *Pollock-plenty-place;* or, as given by an Indian chief, *Pollock-catch-'em-good-many.* The abundance of this kind of fish in this bay still continues.

PEMAQUID.—This name of a harbor and river, with the adjoining territory, appears as early as 1607, in the journal of the Popham colony during its continuance at the mouth of the Kennebec. It has been written in many other forms; but all are easily resolvable into this. It is compounded of *pemi*, *crooked* or *winding*, *ahki*, *land*, place, and *it*, a locative; *pem-ahk-it*, representing *At the Crooked River*, and describing the boundaries of the water, in its tidal portion, by the shores rather than the water itself. Its characteristic "crooked" is marked in contrast with the neighboring John's Bay, which goes out straight to the ocean. In pronunciation the sound of *u* or *w* has been introduced for smoothness. It has been given as *Pemacquid*, *Pemakuit*, and by the Penobscot Indians is called *Pemahkwēduc.*

The history of this place can be given only in the merest outline in a brief note, and need not be attempted, as it is to be furnished in an ample volume.[10]

---

[1] Archer and Brereton's Relations, 3d ser., Mass. H. Coll., pp. 73, 85, 86.

[2] This last appears in Mason's Will, Williamson; I, 267. Hazard, I, 385, 393.

[3] Me. H. Coll., II, 86.

[4] Hist. Me., I, 55.

[5] Josselyn's Two Voyages, 3d ser., Mass. H. Coll., III, 347.

[6] Râle, "Viser." [7] *Pahsukus*, Barratt'sL ist.

[8] *Pestum*, pollock, *acadie*, place of plenty.

[9] *Pascatum*, pollock. Barratt's pamphlet, taken from Nicola Tenesles. *Pascodum* is given by Sabine.

[10] By Professor John Johnston, LL. D., of the college at Middletown, Connecticut, a native of Pemaquid, now embraced in the town of Bristol.

It may be proper to state that the entrance of this river presented a safe harbor for the many fishermen who were on this coast from Europe as early as 1602, (see Neddock,) and with great frequency afterward. There is great probability that settlements were made here and in its neighborhood before 1620. The late author of the history of Portland considered that the patent granted to John Peirce, in June, 1621, had reference to a settlement made hereabouts, and not to that at Plymouth, for which it has been claimed.[1]

The earliest occupation here, of which no known record exists, appears to have been made on the west side of the inner harbor, on Lewis' Point, where cellars, a paved street, a well, the remains of a tan-yard, and the scoria of a blacksmith's shop have been found; as also the indications of a small fortification and terraced grounds about it. When the place grew in importance and demanded greater protection, the inhabitants appear to have removed to the other side of the bay, nearer the ocean, and placed their habitations and defenses on the high part of the peninsula, now known as Fort Hill; having a commanding position on all sides. Here are found beneath the surface, and at one place on the surface, paved streets, in good preservation, and cellars sufficiently numerous to warrant the tradition of a population at one time amounting to five hundred persons. Articles of various kinds of household implements, and those of the artisan, as well as some for military use, have been here exhumed. The well-protected cemetery has preserved some ancient and quaint inscriptions on the grave-stones, while it is said that many of the most ancient have been thrown over the bank to make room for cultivation.

The wars of the French and Indians against the English required the erection of forts for the security of the residents, which, when one after another was captured and destroyed, were probably placed on the spot where the foundation and part of the wall of the last still remain. The date of the building of the first was in 1630. This was destroyed a few years after by a noted pirate, Dixie Bull, who was in 1631, before he had revealed his character, of so good esteem in England as to be a partner with Ferdinando Gorges, 2d, and several others, in a grant of 12,000 acres of land and more at Agamenticus, (York.[2]) The second fort was erected in 1677, under Governor Andros, and called Fort Charles, and was under the control of the government of New York. It was taken and destroyed, with the neighboring dwellings, by a large body of Penobscot Indians, coming from Castine, in 1689. The next fort, called William Henry, was built in 1692, by Sir William Phips, governor of Massachusetts, to whose authority the right of soil here had previously been ceded. This was captured by the French under Iberville, who planted his mortars on the high grounds on the opposite side of the harbor, and thus compelled a surrender. The last fort was erected by Governor Dunbar, in 1729, called Fort Frederick, and remained till the war of the American Revolution, when it was taken down by a vote of the town, lest it should be occupied by the British to the injury of the cause of liberty. A single farm-house is all the dwelling now remaining, and probably built since the construction of the last fort.

The importance of this place, which bore the name of the "city of Jamestown," may be seen in this extract from an old document in the archives of New York, in which the residents here petition "that Pemaquid may still remain the metropolitan of these parts, because it ever have been so before Boston was settled."

PEMETIQ' the name of a place on Mount Desert.

PENOBSCOT.—The particular locality bearing this name originally has been thought to have denoted the rocky bluff on which the light-house stands at the entrance of Castine Bay, northeast of which is the present township of that name. The meaning is easy to be ascertained, from *penops*, *rock*, and *cot*, one of the locative terminations. The name "Rockland" is a perfect representation of the word, which has been extended by usage to denote a river, bay, county, and town. But a better origin may be found in the word *Pănăwămpskik*, or, as more closely pronounced by the present Indians, *Pănwâpskĭk*, long used to denote the "Rocky Falls" and the island near by, on which their village is placed, at Oldtown. The change to the now common name of the river is easily accounted for by the usage of the English visitors on the coast. As early as 1607 the narrative of Popham's colony calls it Penobscot, and in 1614 Smith wrote it much in the present form, *Penobskot*, as the name of a place changed by Prince Charles to *Aborden*, which, as placed on his map, appears to be about the position of Castine. The Indians cling to the ancient name and confine its application to the place of the tribal home. They designate the river, not by one name,

[1] Willis' Hist. Portland, Ed. 1865, pp. 22–23.

[2] Records of the Council in New England, March 2, 1631, compared with December 2, 1631.

but by several, descriptive of its several parts, as *Baamtuguaitook*, *Chimsiticook*, *Ahguazedic*, and others.

Piscataqua.—This river, the boundary between Maine and New Hampshire, was known to Champlain, in 1605, as *Pescadouet*, not very unlike the name as written by Levett, 1623, *Pascattaway*, and to John Smith, in 1614, as *Passataquack;* and in later days, as *Pascataquack*, and similar sounding forms, suggesting a combination, under English treatment, of parts of these two early names; and also the probability that, as in other instances, the different localities on the river were known by different distinctive words, according to their characteristics, thus leading strangers to apply sometimes one, and sometimes another, and again intermingling the two.[1] Kancamagus, (*i. e.* John Hawkins,) sachem of the Pennacooks, in writing to Governor Cranfield, in 1685, said that his grandfather had lived "at place called Malamaki (Merrimac) rever, other name chef Natukkog and Panukkog, that one rever great many names."

The first of these names being traced to *pesketegove*,[2] well denotes the *divided* character of the sea-ward portion of this stream, in which unite Spruce Creek, Back River connected with Great Bay, and the Piscasset or Lamprey River. The other name has been derived from *pos* or *pâs*, *great*, *attuck*, *deer*, and *auke*, or *ahki*, *place*, with *w* euphonic, making *Pâs-attuck-wak*, *Big-Deer place;* and probably denoting the territory on the interior portions of this stream. The same words enter into the composition of *Pautuckaway*. In regard to this word, applied to one of the inland ranges of mountains in New Hampshire, it is related that in colonial times, when the inhabitants in that district had become numerous enough to petition for an act of incorporation as a town, they sent by their agents a *large deer*, caught within its proposed limits, as a present to the governor, Benning Wentworth, who thereupon signified his wish that the new town should be called "Deerfield," thus bearing a name indicative of the gift. Henceforth it took the place of *Pautuckaway*, of which it is a good representation.

Presumpscot.—This word shows how the tendencies of the early settlers led them to make it conform to some better known English word. Here they adopted the idea of the word *presumption*. There are several modes of writing it, and *Pesumpscot* comes the nearest to the true form, which, divided into its parts, presents *Pes*,[3] *much*, *omp*, from *wompi*, *clear*, *shallow*, where the bottom can be *seen*, and *cot*, a locative. The meaning will be *Many-Shallows-River*, corresponding to the many *rips* found in its course, or, as the Indian "sangman" (governor) at Oldtown explained it, *Rough-places River*

Pumgustic.—The falls at the mouth of the "Wescustogo," or Royal's River, in Yarmouth.

Pomkoostook.—*Mud-stream-place*, from the *mud-flats* just below.

Purpooduc.—Spring Point on Cape Elizabeth;[4] but was used to denote the neighboring territory. The meaning is not known. It has been thought to refer to a *burying-place*, from the Micmac *Pulpooduck*.

Quohog.—A bay, on the shores of which were and are found the round clam, denoted *Poquauhock*, by R. Williams, and Pekwâhak, by Râle. Both these words are in the plural form. See Hog Island.

Rosier.—A cape so designated from its wild rose-bushes on its rocky shores; from the French.

Sábino, also Sebénoa, the last two vowels coalescing as in *oak*, and often uniting in Strachey's History, where these names are first found, as in *roap*, *shoare*. The true form would be *Sebéno*. It was the name of a province called by the Indians Sabino, so called of a Sagamo or chief commander under the grand Bassaba. He claimed to be "lord of the river Sachadehoc."[5] The word appears to have a near connection with *sebe*, a river. The explanation by the Indians is, "where a river makes into the land." As a locality it would apply to *Atkins' Bay*, and may be called *The Bay of the River*. The name has been given to a headland near the mouth of the Kennebec. The sachem may have derived it from the place.

Saco.—This name, like Sakunk in the Delaware dialect, from the root *sâk*, outlet, and the locative *o* for *oke*, denotes the mouth of the river. The word by which this river was known to

[1] Belknap's Hist. N. H., Farmer's Ed., 509.
[2] Trumbull's Ind. Geog. Names, pp. 10, 11.
[3] *Pesangwi*, *much*, *Beaucoup*, Râle.
[4] Willis' Hist. Portland, 96, 191.
[5] Strachey's Hist. Trav., Cap. IX, 18; X, 26.

Lescarbot and Biard is *Chouacöet*, (pron. shwâ-co-et,) and probably had a connection with the falls a few miles above its mouth; more names than one not being unusual to mark a stream. The word *m'sooahq*, meaning *dead*, dry, as applied to *wood*, followed by *kooe*, *pine-tree*, and the locative *et*, gives *m'soo-ah-koo-et;* easily changed by the French writers to the word presented above. The pines, once abundant there, may have been burned, like the forests around the *Skootak*, (Fire land Lakes,) and the adjoining territory, thus desolated, may have originated the idea of *The dead-pine-falls*. The oldest reported word of the harder utterance yielded to the easier, and *Saco* now denotes the river, falls, and city.

SAGADAHOC.—This name is thus written in Popham's Latin letter to the King, in 1607. It is derived from *sanktai-i-wi*, to finish, and *onk*, a locative, that is, the *finishing place;* where a river ceases to be a river. It means *the mouth of a river;* but was applied geographically by the Indians to indicate the mouth of the Kennebec, which alone of the large rivers preserves its character of a river till it reaches the ocean. The original form would be *Sank-ta-onk*. Purchas places the name in the mouth. It is written with nearly sixty variations,[1] in some of which the first syllable *sank* is preserved. Near its mouth Popham's colony, in 1607, built their Fort St. George.

SASANOA.—The name of an Indian, who is proved, by a careful examination of Rosier's narrative of Weymouth's voyage to the Kennebec, compared with Strachey's account of the same and of the Popham colony, and with Gorges' "Brief Narration," to have been a chief of distinction, closely related to the Bashaba, whose name, as appears in Strachey and Purchas, was applied to a by-river of some note, meaning the inland passage by water from the Kennebec to the Sheepscot, and by Smith to Agamenticus.

SEBASCODEGAN.—Great island in Harpswell. Among the several variations occurs the early form of *Chebascodiggin*. *K'tche* is *great; t'bascodegan*[2] in Penobscot is a *measure*. This solution of the name shows that the natives had taken some means of *measuring* the island, and had found it *great*.

SEGUIN, in Strachey's account of the Popham colony, is called *Sutquin*.[3] Smith says *Sagadahoc* is known by Satquin and four or five isles at its mouth.[4] The meaning is not ascertained. The present name is a Spanish word.

SHEEPSCOT is derived from *seep*, a *bird*, *sis*, *little*, *a* euphonic, and *cot*, a locative. In the Etchemin dialect *seep* is *duck*. *Seepsisacot* is *Little-bird-place*. The well-marked tradition is that the Indians annually, at the proper season, resorted to this river for the purpose of taking the *young ducks*, which were found in great plenty there.

SISQUISIC.—Cousin's River, Yarmouth.

SKILLINGS, from a family of that name.[5]

SMALL POINT.—Levett, 1623, calls it the "Cape of Sagadahoc." On an ancient map, in India ink, of the Kennebec and the adjoining territory, made by John Small, surveyor, it is called by the present name. The "Small" family was resident in the neighborhood for many years, probably at or near "Small Point Harbor." A field-book of another survey of the Kennebec, made about a century ago, is preserved in the library of the Maine Historical Society.

SPURWINK.—A stream in Scarboro', of which the name has some resemblance to an English local name.

ST. GEORGE'S RIVER.—The name St. George was given by Popham to Monhegan; and after this island became known by its original name, it was transferred to the islands and river now thus denoted.

SUSQUESONG.—Cousin's Island, Yarmouth.

---

[1] On Johnson's Map of 1754, dedicated to Governor Shirley, this name is given to the *Amorescoggin*, (*Androscoggin*,) as the principal of two alternate names, with the remark that it was "so called by Mr. Pople."[t] Sagadahoc R., so called by Mons. Bellin, and also by most or all the ancient plans "Strachey's account of the Popham colony speaks only of this and Pemaquid Rivers, and mentions Gilbert's going with an expedition for the head of the river Sachadehoc," Chap. X. All the indications of his narrative point to the present Androscoggin, and the name being thus applied in Johnson's Map is confirmatory of the traditional use of this appellation.

[2] In Râle, *Tebakoonigan*, "une mesure."

[3] Me. H. Coll., III, 298.

[4] Mass. H. C., 3d ser., VI, 120.

[5] Willis' Hist. Portland, Index.

---

[t] Me. Hist. Col., Vol. III, 329, printed Popple. He held an office in the Plantation Office, Whitehall, London.

TOLAM.—The aboriginal name for Falmouth,[1] embracing Portland.

TOWESSIC, and, without the locative, *Towass*,[2] is a point in Woolwich that lies over against the upper end of Arrowsic Island.[3] The Indian explanation refers the meaning to "breaking through." This idea will suit the fact that the by-river of some note called "Sasanoa," in the account of the Popham colony,[4] here passes through a broken place in the high walls of the Kennebec. Perhaps it may be translated "*The Broken Passage.*"

TUNK, applied to a mountain in Hancock County; also to a pond. It appears to be the end of a word, as it is in *Carritunk*. As the mountain is called "Big" and the pond "Great," the Indian name may have been in correspondence with these descriptions; for which *K'tche-t-unk* (Chetunk) will be the appropriate word.

WAUKEAG.—Neck, in Frenchman's Bay. This may have been *Wamkeag, i. e., Wamkik.* The name may have been taken from *wampi*,[5] *clear, shallow,* (*water,*) and *kik*, a locative, from shallow water near it, and may represent "Shallow Bay."

WANSQUEAK,[6] harbor in Goldsboro'.

WASS is an English surname,[7] now known in the eastern part of the State.

WEBHANNET is the Indian name of the town of Wells; from *web*,[8] a *wife, hanne*, a *stream*, and *et*, a locative; and may find its representative in *wife-river*. A similar appliance of this feminine relation may be seen in *Squawagusset, Squawhan, Squawkeag.*

This explanation is illustrated by the fact that about 1649 Chabinoke devised to John Wadleigh "all his interest in Nampscascoke, being the larger part of Wells, on the condition of the annual allowance of a bushel of corn to the 'Old Webb,' (*i. e.*, wife,) his mother."[9]

WESCUSTOGO.—Royal's River in Yarmouth. The analysis of this word resolves it into *Kowass-koos-togue-oke, Pine-stream-trout-place;* all which describe facts once true. The first syllable has been dropped.

WESKEAG is said to mean Grassy River. But if it be an abbreviation for *Kowasskik*, then it will be Pine River; *ko* being dropped.

WHISKEAG, also in a Pejepscot map written *Worsqueage*, suggesting *Kowasskik*, with the same meaning as in the last definition, *k* being lost in English pronunciation. It is a small stream on the west side of the Kennebec, and is regarded as the third of the "runs of water" passed over by Waymouth and his party in his exploration in 1605, and mentioned in Rosier's Narrative as "the farthest and last we passed," which "ran with a great stream able to drive a mill," as it now does. Pines once abounded here.

WINCHEAG BAY, east of Mount Desert, where M. Cadillac lived.[10] *Winne, beautiful, k'tche, great, ag* or *ak*, a locative.

WICHACOWICK, the name applied to Ellsworth River and Falls. This word is of the like composition with the others dependent on the *Pines*. In one of the cognate dialects a word is found written *witsh-wock-ak*, explained as *pine-nuts*, which must be the *cones*; *ak* denoting the plural. Thus, this name will be *witsch*, *a* euphonic, *kooé*, or *co, pine, ick*, locative, *Place of Pine-tree cones*, or, more awkwardly, *Cones of Pine place.*

WISCASSET, called by the Indians *Wichcasset*, has been thought to mean "the confluence of three waters." But there is nothing in the composition of the word to sustain the definition. The same may be said of "the place of springs." Its origin is like that of the last word. *Witschkowass*, plural of *koé, et*, locative; Wichkwass-*et, Place of Pine-Tree Cones*, or Pine-cones-place.

---

[1] J. De Laet, quoted by Williamson, I, 39.

[2] Or *Towess.*

[3] Pejepscot Papers, Vol. I, 121, called *Towasset Bay*, (Back Bay;) Williamson, II, 347, as a boundary of Woolwich. The syllables *et* and *ic* have a similar meaning.

[4] Strachey, Caput X, Sept 27th.

[5] *Umbagog* has a similar origin in *womp-be* from *nebe, water, g* euphonic, *og* or *ok*, a locative, *i. e., Shallow Lake*, corresponding with the fact.

[6] This may have been *Wompskeag*, with a meaning like the preceding.

[7] Willis' Portland, 321.

[8] Woods' N. E. Prospect.

[9] Folsom's Saco., p. 120.

[10] Williamson, I, 588; note.

www.ingramcontent.com/pod-product-compliance
Lightning Source LLC
LaVergne TN
LVHW020640110826
845149LV00004B/1294

9781418190798